BELFAST

HISTORY TOUR

ACKNOWLEDGEMENTS

I am very grateful to the following for providing access to old photograph and postcard archives: *Belfast Telegraph*; J. J. Bonar Holmes; Belfast Central Library; Elizabeth Lowry; Lallie Dean; East Belfast Historical Society; Michael McMullan; Mike Maybin; and my mother, Edith Campbell (née Walker), who married my father, Revd A. J. E. Campbell, at St George's Church, High Street, Belfast. Also thanks to Chris Woods for diligent proofreading and to Blue Badge tourist guide Sue McKay for many wonderful insights and suggestions.

First published 2020

Amberley Publishing
The Hill, Stroud,
Gloucestershire, GL5 4EP
www.amberley-books.com

Copyright © Aidan Campbell, 2020.
Map contains LPS data using Ordnance
Survey of Northern Ireland datasets
under Open Government Licence v3.0.

The right of Aidan Campbell to be
identified as the Author of this work
has been asserted in accordance with
the Copyrights, Designs and Patents
Act 1988.

ISBN 978 1 3981 0185 2 (print)
ISBN 978 1 3981 0186 9 (ebook)

British Library Cataloguing in
Publication Data.
A catalogue record for this book is
available from the British Library.

Origination by Amberley Publishing.
Printed in Great Britain.

INTRODUCTION

In 1575 the Earl of Essex wrote 'I resolve not to build but at one place; namely at Belfast.' The modern history of Belfast (Beal Feirste in Irish, meaning 'mouth of the sandbank ford', or Bilfawst in Ulster Scots) dates back to 1613 when Sir Arthur Chichester was granted Belfast Castle, much of the surrounding land and a charter from James I that created a corporate borough or town. Belfast has the distinction of being the only town in Ireland to be owned by one family, the Chichesters, later the Earls and finally the Marquises of Donegall. (Not Donegal as in the county, but Donegall as the result of a clerical error.) Their influence in the early days of Belfast remains in numerous places and thoroughfares that bear the names of family members. Some examples include Chichester, Donegall, Shaftesbury, Franklin, Glengall, Arthur, Catherine, Amelia, Eliza and Charlotte.

Belfast made the transition from small market town to provincial capital. The population of Belfast grew substantially from 1800 when there were only 20,000 inhabitants to 1901 when the population was 349,000. In 1888 Belfast was granted a city charter by Queen Victoria and the role of mayor was elevated to that of lord mayor. Belfast had become the third largest port in the United Kingdom and generated customs revenues only exceeded by London and Liverpool.

This tour begins at Stormont, the seat of the devolved government of Northern Ireland in the outer reaches of east Belfast, and travels toward Belfast city centre, looking at the centre of old Belfast town through our built heritage and how it extended into south Belfast during the Victorian and Edwardian period.

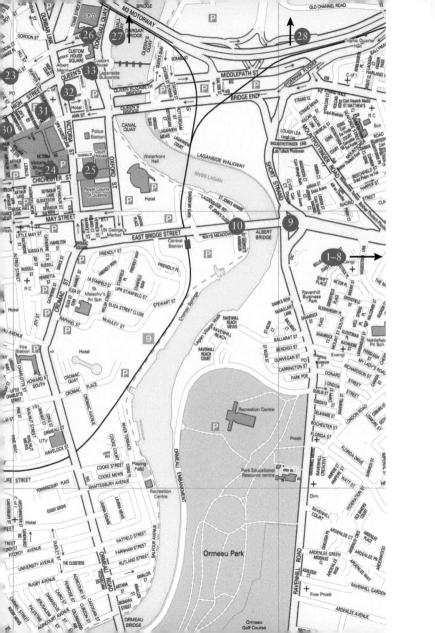

KEY

1. Stormont Castle
2. Stormont Parliament Buildings
3. Campbell College
4. Ormiston
5. Craigavon
6. St Mark's Dundela
7. Belmont Presbyterian Church
8. St Colmcille's
9. Albert Bridge
10. East Bridge Street
11. White Linen Hall
12. Belfast City Hall
13. Donegall Square – Edward Harland Statue
14. Donegall Square North
15. Donegall Square East
16. Donegall Square South and West
17. Donegall Place
18. Castle Place
19. Royal Avenue Upper
20. Royal Avenue Lower
21. Donegall Street – Poor House
22. Donegall Street – St Anne's Cathedral
23. Exchange or Assembly Rooms
24. Victoria Square
25. Belfast Town Hall
26. Custom House
27. Harbour Office
28. Harland & Wolff Shipyard
29. Castle Place Bank Buildings
30. Castle Junction
31. High Street
32. St George's Church, High Street
33. Albert Memorial
34. Wellington Place
35. Royal Belfast Academical Institution
36. Presbyterian Assembly Buildings
37. Grand Opera House
38. Great Northern Railway Station
39. Shaftesbury Square
40. Crescent Arts Centre
41. Union Theological College
42. Queen's University
43. Botanic Gardens Entrance
44. Methodist College
45. Ulster Museum
46. Palm House Botanic Gardens
47. Friar's Bush Graveyard
48. The Workhouse
49. King's Hall, Balmoral
50. Shaw's Bridge

1. STORMONT CASTLE

Stormont Castle is a mansion on the Stormont estate used as the main meeting place of the Northern Ireland Executive. It was built in the Scottish Baronial style in 1858, set in a large wooded demesne and reputed to replicate Balmoral Castle, Scotland. Stormont Castle replaced a previous Georgian house called 'Storm Mount' owned by the Cleland family whose home this was until the 1890s. Following the Government of Ireland Act in 1920 the 235-acre Stormont Castle demesne was acquired as the new Parliament Buildings site for the government of Northern Ireland.

2. STORMONT PARLIAMENT BUILDINGS

From 1921 the new Northern Ireland Parliament had been based firstly at Belfast City Hall and then the Presbyterian Assembly's College, Botanic Avenue. The new Parliament was seeking a permanent home and early front runners were large mansions at Belfast Castle, Belvoir and Orangefield before Stormont was finally chosen. The foundation stone was laid at a grand ceremonial occasion on

19 May 1928. Parliament Buildings (although singular in execution, it is described as plural in nomenclature) Stormont was beginning to take its familiar shape in this early 1930s photograph, and the original architect's plans included a great dome on the roof. The layout of Parliament Buildings follows that of the UK Parliament at Westminster. It is designed in the Greek classical tradition and constructed from English Portland stone.

3. CAMPBELL COLLEGE

The trustees of linen merchant Henry Campbell received instructions that his fortune should be used to build either a hospital or school to bear his name, and a school was agreed on: 'A College for the purpose of giving there a superior liberal Protestant education.' The main gate lodge at Campbell College was designed in the Tudor revival style by William Henry Lynn and is now a listed building. It was described by one pupil as being like 'a claret-label chateau'. This is the way it looked in 1900 shortly after completion. Author C. S. Lewis was a pupil at Campbell College in autumn 1910, only a mile from his home 'Little Lea' on Circular Road. A more recent pupil was Gary Lightbody of Snow Patrol, apparently inspired by the poetry of Seamus Heaney.

4. ORMISTON

Ormiston was built in 1867 in the Scottish Baronial style for James Combe, a Scots-born ironfounder and linen manufacturer whose business was called Combe-Barbour. At the very pinnacle of Edwardian society, its main entrance was on Belmont Road where a gate lodge still remains. In 1876 the grounds comprised 62 acres and

were owned by Harland & Wolff (shipbuilders), Sir Edward Harland and then Lord William Pirrie, who apparently lavishly entertained in a dining room capable of seating 160 guests. Ormiston was acquired in 1927 by Campbell College as a junior boarding school, then in the 1970s by the Police Authority and more recently by a local businessman who has lovingly restored it as a private home.

5. CRAIGAVON

Craigavon House is set in a demesne originally extending to 20 acres and built in 1870 for whiskey distiller James Craig, the father of Sir James Craig, the first prime minister of Northern Ireland. It was at Craigavon in 1911 that Sir Edward Carson and Captain James Craig organised a huge protest demonstration against home rule, involving 50,000 men, which led to the formation of the Ulster Volunteer Force. In 1915 Craigavon was made available to UVF hospitals for sick and wounded soldiers from the First World War. In the 1990s a new Somme Nursing Home was constructed nearby to replace the old UVF Hospital.

6. ST MARK'S DUNDELA

St Mark's Church of Ireland, Dundela, is located on Holywood Road at the junction with Sydenham Avenue and stands in a prominent position, where its 150-foot-tall bell tower provides a very conspicuous landmark. According to folklore this hill, 'Bunker's Hill', took its name from the site of a famous battle from the American Revolutionary War in 1775. St Mark's Church was consecrated in 1878 and the first rector was Revd Thomas Robert Hamilton, whose daughter Flora married Albert Lewis. They had a family of two boys: Warnie and his younger brother Clive Staples, or C. S. Lewis, who would go on to author *The Chronicles of Narnia*. The old rectory door knocker is in the style of a lion's head, which no doubt served as inspiration for Aslan the lion.

7. BELMONT PRESBYTERIAN CHURCH

Thomas McClure was a wealthy tobacco merchant and politician who bought a vast tract of land in east Belfast in 1858 from the estate of Lord Ranfurley. Thomas McClure (made a baronet in 1874) lived at a mansion called Belmont, which included a 100-acre demesne that was acquired for the new Campbell College in 1894. He was an elder in Fisherwick Presbyterian Church in the centre of Belfast and complained that the long journey home from church kept him late for lunch. So, in 1859, he provided a site for a new church, Belmont Presbyterian Church (pictured here), which was opened for worship on Sunday 26 January 1862.

8. ST COLMCILLE'S

The foundation stone of St Colmcille's Roman Catholic Church at Ballyhackamore was laid by the Most Revd Dr Henry, Bishop of Down and Connor, on 25 August 1907. The new church was dedicated on Sunday 25 July 1909, when this photograph was probably taken. The Blitz of 1941 did quite some damage to the area and destroyed the new parochial hall at St Colmcille's (only built in 1937) as well as levelling St Joseph's National School, though fortunately the church survived. The building to the far left, just across the Upper Newtownards Road, is the Royal Irish Constabulary barracks.

R. C. Chapel, Ballyhackamore.

9. ALBERT BRIDGE

The Lagan Bridge, or Halfpenny Bridge, collapsed in 1886. An eyewitness to the tragedy was sixteen-year-old Billy Reid, who remarked 'we had hardly gone a dozen yards when there was an almighty crash and we all ran back to find the bridge had collapsed ... aye the poor 'oul watchman went down with it'. The new Albert Bridge was opened in 1890. The prominent building to the right is Albertbridge Congregational Church on Short Strand, which was something of a landmark as it had an illuminated sign that bore a scriptural message. This church building was demolished in 1985 and a new one built at neighbouring Woodstock Link.

10. EAST BRIDGE STREET

Crossing the Albert Bridge in 1900, travelling to Belfast city centre, the road becomes East Bridge Street and on the corner of Laganbank Road was the municipal electricity works and offices, described as 'late baroque' in architectural style. This power station opened in 1898, on the same day the foundation stone for Belfast City Hall was laid, and was built to supply the needs of the growing city and the electrification of the horse-drawn tramway system, which was completed in 1905. The last of the power station buildings were demolished in the 1980s to be replaced by an office block, although the white gate posts have been thoughtfully retained.

11. WHITE LINEN HALL

The linen industry was a major feature of Belfast's commercial life during the eighteenth century, and in 1784 the White Linen Hall (seen here) was erected at Donegall Square. It enabled local linen producers to market and export their wares. By 1888 Belfast Corporation sought to buy the site for a city hall as the existing town hall in Victoria Street was no longer large enough. The owner of this site was the Countess of Shaftesbury, who was keen that 'the whole space thus made available be laid out as a public garden' but was eventually persuaded that Donegall Square could accommodate both the City Hall and public gardens in the grounds.

12. BELFAST CITY HALL

Following a competition, the architect chosen for Belfast City Hall was Alfred Brumwell Thomas, who had designed town halls for Stockport, Woolwich and Clacton. Funded in part by the profits of the municipal gas industry, the Lord Lieutenant of Ireland, Lord Cadogan, laid the foundation stone in 1898 and during construction the builders H&J Martin were asked to erect hoarding around the site as there were complaints that building work was frightening horses and injuring the public. At the opening ceremony in 1906 Lord Aberdeen remarked, 'The massiveness of this noble structure typifies the sure and stable foundations of the prosperity and welfare of this great city'.

13. DONEGALL SQUARE – EDWARD HARLAND STATUE

Edward Harland was an important figure in the story of Belfast shipbuilding. Originally from Scarborough, he came to Belfast to work at Robert Hickson's shipyard, which he eventually bought and entered into partnership with Gustav Wolff to form Harland & Wolff in 1861. He was chairman of Belfast Harbour Commissioners in 1875, made a baronet in 1885 and became Mayor of Belfast, retired from the shipyard in 1889 and in the same year he served as MP for north Belfast. He died in 1895 and his white marble statue (seen here) was the first to be erected in 1903 at Belfast City Hall, which was still under construction.

14. DONEGALL SQUARE NORTH

A 1946 view of the front of Belfast City Hall from Donegall Square North looking in the direction of Chichester Street and several of the grand old buildings from Victorian and Edwardian times survive. On the right is the Ocean Accident Insurance Buildings (1902) and on the left is Richardson Sons & Owden's linen headquarters (1869) – now occupied by Marks & Spencer. The tall building to the far left (1888) was Robinson & Cleaver's department store, which contained the very latest technological innovations such as electric lighting and 'a luxurious passenger elevator'. Prestigious customers included 'The Queen, Maharajah of Cooch Behar and the Emporer and Empress of Germany'. Burger King now occupies the ground floor.

15. DONEGALL SQUARE EAST

The proximity of Belfast City Hall (left) to Robinson & Cleaver's department store (centre) and the Richardson Sons & Owden's premises (right) from Donegall Square East is evident in this 1928 scene. The hub of local car retailing was near Belfast City Hall as recently as the 1970s, but the showrooms have since moved to the Boucher Road area of south Belfast. The proliferation of parked cars are from the motor garage and showrooms of Harry Ferguson Ltd, which are just out of site to the right alongside Donegall Square Methodist Church. This church was designed by architect Isaac Farrell (great-great-great-great-uncle of tourist guide Sue McKay). In 1909 Harry Ferguson became the first Irishman to make a powered aeroplane flight. He is also remembered for his role in the development of the modern agricultural tractor.

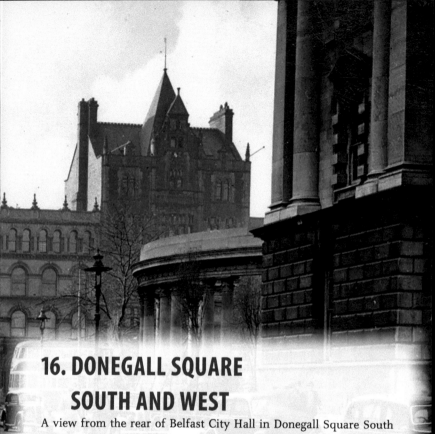

16. DONEGALL SQUARE SOUTH AND WEST

A view from the rear of Belfast City Hall in Donegall Square South looking across to Donegall Square West in 1942. The tall five-storey building is the Northern Bank, designed by architects Young & Mackenzie and built in the late Gothic Revival style in 1903, once providing 'an exceptionally attractive and romantic skyline, especially at dusk'. It was eventually demolished, along with the Venetain linen warehouse next door, for a new bank headquarters in 1970. In the distance looking along Howard Street is Presbyterian Assembly Buildings, which opened in 1905 and was also designed by Young & Mackenzie.

17. DONEGALL PLACE

Donegall Place extends from Belfast City Hall to Castle Place and the early centre of Belfast. This street was laid out in the 1780s as part of town improvements by landowner Lord Donegall, whose name, along with other family members, crops up frequently in Belfast street naming. By the 1800s Donegall Place was the most desirable residential area in Belfast. It was in the 1850s, following the Great Famine, that the grand terraced houses became retail and other business premises and the wealthy business owners and middle classes moved out of the city centre and built grand villas on the hills around Belfast. Notice the light road traffic in this early 1900s view.

18. CASTLE PLACE

When Donegall Place was built it was a largely residential area for the great and the good of society and even the landlords, the Donegall family, lived in a house here. Their home was on the corner with Donegall Square and eventually became the Royal Hotel at which authors Charles Dickens and Thackery once stayed. In this 1920s view of Donegall Place from Castle Place, Belfast City Hall looms large in the distance. It looks like a busy shopping day for some of the leading department stores of the time including the Bank Buildings (right) and Anderson & McAuley (centre), which have both ceased trading.

19. ROYAL AVENUE UPPER

Royal Avenue begins at Castle Place and continues to Donegall Street. It was opened up in around 1880 and the aim was to create a much grander and more dignified thoroughfare with regular building lines and façades, as this 1900 scene demonstrates. The white building on the left is the Provincial Bank (1867), now Tesco Metro, and just beyond the first building with the cupola is the Ulster Reform Club (1885). The second cupola belongs to 'Belfast's largest and most luxurious' Grand Central Hotel (1893) and its guests included Winston Churchill, Al Jolson and the Lone Ranger (who wore his mask at mealtimes). It became an army base in 1972 and was demolished in the 1980s for the new Castlecourt shopping centre.

20. ROYAL AVENUE LOWER

The Belfast Free Library (now Central Library) is the large classical building (centre) that has a Dumfries red sandstone exterior. It opened in 1888 on the day that Belfast was granted city status. The Central Library recently had a starring role in acclaimed BBC drama *Line of Duty* when it doubled as police headquatres. Just beyond the library, the offices of the *Belfast Telegraph* were opened in 1886 and a contemporary description was of 'the most imposing exterior of any newspaper office in Ireland'. During the Second World War, *Stars & Stripes* newspaper was instigated by President Roosevelt as a morale booster for American troops fighting overseas and published locally by the *Belfast Telegraph*, which relocated to new premises at Clarendon Dock in 2016.

21. DONEGALL STREET – POOR HOUSE

The Belfast Charitable Society was the city's first charitable voluntary organisation. It was established in 1752 to provide relief for the destitute. Early minutes of the society record: 'A poor-house and hospital are greatly wanted in Belfast for the support of vast numbers of real objects of charity in this parish, for the employment of idle beggars who crowd to it from all parts of the North, and for the

reception of infirm and diseased poor.' In those pre-welfare state times local landowner Lord Donegall provided an 8-acre plot of ground at what is now No. 2 North Queen Street and was given the role of president during his lifetime. The Poor House, or Clifton House, was opened in 1774 and Mary Ann McCracken was a key figure in its development. Today it houses a heritage centre alongside a residential home and sheltered accommodation apartments.

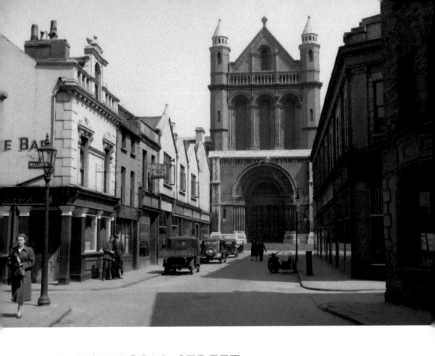

22. DONEGALL STREET –
ST ANNE'S CATHEDRAL

The old Church of Ireland parish church of St Anne was built on Donegall Street (at Lord Donegall's expense) in 1776. The church was named after the biblical mother of Mary but was also coincidentally the name of the 5th Earl of Donegall's wife. It was replaced by St Anne's Cathedral (seen here in 1952), which was consecrated in 1904, although building work has continued over the past 100 years or so and it escaped the Blitz in 1941. At the time of construction it was the fourth new cathedral to be built in the British Isles since the Reformation. The dean of St Anne's from 1926 to 1932 was the Very Revd Henry Robert Brett, great-uncle of this author.

23. EXCHANGE OR ASSEMBLY ROOMS

The earliest public building survivng in Belfast is the Exchange or Assembly Rooms. It was constructed as a single-storey market house in 1769 by landlord Lord Donegall and is located in an area known as the 'Four Corners' – the junction of Bridge Steet, Waring Street, Donegall Street and North Street. It was extended in 1776 by the addition of a second storey known as the Assembly Rooms. An historic building, it was once used for discussion (and rejection) of Belfast's involvement in the slave trade and as a courthouse in the trials of members of the United Irishmen following the 1798 Rebellion. Then in 1845 it became a branch of the Belfast Bank, and it now lies empty awaiting redevelopment under the proposed Tribeca scheme.

24. VICTORIA SQUARE

When Victoria Street was opened in the 1840s it was known as Cow Lane and Victoria Square as Poultry Square, but when Queen Victoria made a royal visit to Belfast in 1849 the grander names were adopted. Victoria Square was once the home of the town morgue, Town Hall and Finlay's soap works. A supply of clean drinking water was a problem in Belfast years ago, so in 1852 the aerated mineral water company Cantrell & Cochrane Ltd was established (in the old Town Hall – look closely) and an artesian well was sunk to tap into the underground Cromac Spring. Sparkling beverages were then exported around the world. Victoria Square shopping centre was opened on this site in 2008.

25. BELFAST TOWN HALL

A new Town Hall for Belfast was opened 1870 and described as being 'of sturdy brick construction in mixed elements of a Venetian gothic style'. It was not admired by everyone – the public mood in Victorian times required a more ostentatious display. Apparently, the architect's inspiration came from drawings made on holiday in Italy. Many people protested and thought the Town Hall 'not a public building'. Consequently, only thirty years later a much grander Belfast City Hall with a domed roof was under construction at Donegall Square. The Town Hall building was used as the Family and Coroners Court for many years but has recently closed.

26. CUSTOM HOUSE

Once described as 'Belfast's finest public building', the Custom House
was designed by architect Charles Lanyon and completed in 1857. It
once housed the Inland Revenue and the post office, where writer
Anthony Trollope was once employed and is commemorated by an

Ulster History Circle blue plaque. In this 1928 view a close look will reveal a cannon beside the front door, which was captured from the Russians in the Crimean War. A high point in Belfast as a trading port came in 1905 when only the ports of London and Liverpool in the British Isles collected more customs revenue.

27. HARBOUR OFFICE

The Ballast Board was a body constituted in 1785 for the development of Belfast's burgeoning port, including new deep water channels and eventually land reclamation as the city lacked a good natural harbour. In 1847 the Belfast Harbour Act brought the Belfast Harbour Commissioners into being and the new Harbour Office (seen here), designed in the style of an Italian Renaissance palace and finished in brown sandstone, was opened in 1854. It has been described as 'one of the most handsome public buildings in Belfast'. The Belfast Harbour Police was also founded in 1847 to look after the 2,000-acre harbour estate, making it the oldest continuously operating law enforcement agency in Ireland. The small sailing vessels in this 1890s view from Queen's Quay look like either schooners or brigantines, which could well be colliers bringing supplies of coal from Cumbrian or Welsh coalfields.

28. HARLAND & WOLFF SHIPYARD

It is often suggested that shipbuilding in Belfast is the history of one company: Harland & Wolff, who have survived longer than any other and account for 68 per cent of all launches. The *Titanic* is probably the best-known ship launched on 31 May 1911 (seen here) in the presence of Lord Pirrie, J. Pierpoint Morgan and J. Bruce Ismay, plus 100,000 onlookers. Once ranked among the largest shipbuilders in the world, Gustav Wolff remarked 'Sir Edward Harland builds the ships, Mr Pirrie makes the speeches and I smoke the cigars for the firm!' Harland & Wolff's last shipbuilding project was MV *Anvil Point*, which launched in 2003. The company now engages in ship repair and offshore construction projects and the two massive shipyard gantry cranes, Samson and Goliath, survive as buildings of 'architectural or historic interest'.

29. CASTLE PLACE BANK BUILDINGS

There are a couple of versions as to how the Bank Buildings (seen here), located in Castle Place, was named. One is due to its location on the banks of the now culverted River Farset and an alternative is that the original Bank Buildings contained Cunningham's Bank, which opened on this site in 1787 and collapsed financially. By 1853 a wholesale drapery business had been established, which was eventually operated by the firm Robertson, Ledlie, Ferguson & Co., who were described as 'wholesale and retail linen merchants, woollen drapers, silk mercers, general house furnishers, British and foreign warehousemen'. This 1920 view of the imposing Bank Buildings was opened in 1900, but was destroyed in a fire during August 2018 and is currently under reconstruction.

30. CASTLE JUNCTION

The old centre of Belfast town in the 1890s looking along Castle Place to High Street from the Bank Buildings. A great view of a busy Castle Junction, which is not an address but purely a tramway term. On 27 April 1613 James I granted a charter creating a corporate borough for the town and castle of Belfast to Sir Arthur Chichester, then Lord Deputy of Ireland, whose descendants were awarded titles under the Donegall name. The large bow-fronted building (to the left) is the Ulster Club, which was built in 1860, demolished in 1981 and once described as 'a rather hefty slice of Brighton'.

31. HIGH STREET

The original Belfast Castle was located not far from here and burned down in 1708. Castle Place leads on to High Street and follows the irregular course of the River Farset – thus the bend in the road. The name Belfast is taken from Gaelic, 'Beal Feirste', meaning 'mouth of the sandbank ford'. During the early 1700s several bridges spanned the Farset and High Street contained a number of quays, allowing sailing ships to dock. By the late 1800s the street was lined with shops and had changed very little by 1939 (seen here), but most of the grand buildings on the left-hand side of High Street would be destroyed during the Blitz in 1941. In the distance is the Albert Clock.

32. ST GEORGE'S CHURCH, HIGH STREET

St George's Church, High Street, was built in 1816 as a chapel of ease for St Anne's parish church in neighbouring Donegall Street. The four-columned Corinthian porch was acquired from Ballyscullion House near Castledawson. The porch was transported to Belfast in lighters via the Lagan Navigation. St George's was originally named after George III, but ultimately consecrated in the name of the saint. The Chapel of Le Ford, which dated back to the 1300s, was probably located on this site not far from the original Belfast Castle, or motte, on the banks of the River Farset. My parents were married here in 1956.

33. ALBERT MEMORIAL

The Albert Memorial, aka the Albert Clock, is a four-sided clock tower in the (appropriate) German Gothic style. It was built in 1869 as a memorial to the late prince consort whose marble statue stands on a pedestal at the front of the tower and looks along High Street. A scandal developed in 1865 when the design competition was awarded to the second-placed entry, but this decision was eventually sensibly reversed. For many years the 145-foot clock tower leaned to one side and it was commented that 'it had both the time and the inclination!' given its close proximity to houses of ill repute in the docks area.

34. WELLINGTON PLACE

The Municipal Technical Institute, later Belfast Metropolitan College, opened in 1907 and closed in 2013. It was located at College Square North and was known for many years in Belfast as 'the Tech', which has the aim of moulding education to the needs of local industry. Land was acquired from the neighbouring Royal Belfast Academical Institution (in the background here) who sold the site as they were in some debt at the time. The Tech was built in an area known then as the Harley Street of Belfast due to the large number of medical professionals who lived there and complained of the 'vulgar display' presented by the new building.

MUNICIPAL TECHNIC

35. ROYAL BELFAST ACADEMICAL INSTITUTION

Belfast Academical Institution, or Inst, was opened in 1814 'to diffuse useful knowledge, particularly among the middling orders of society'. It is a long three-storey Georgian building in dark red brick with

ROYAL ACADEMICAL INSTITUTION, BELFAST

stone details and has been described as 'by no means distinguished by profusion of ornament'. In 1831, William IV granted Inst a royal title. The school provided the main foundation for the Medical Faculty of the new Queen's College, Belfast, and over 500 doctors were trained at Inst between 1835 and 1849. Known for its sporting prowess, Inst first won the rugby Schools' Cup in 1888 and seventy-eight Instonians have played for Ireland and eleven for the British and Irish Lions.

36. PRESBYTERIAN ASSEMBLY BUILDINGS

Church House is located at Fisherwick Place, which is a continuation of College Square East and home to the General Assembly of the Presbyterian Church in Ireland. It was built in the Gothic style and was opened by the Duke of Argyll. Church House is dominated by a 40-metre-high clock tower, which contains Belfast's only peal of twelve bells. Church House, or Assembly Buildings, was refurbished in 1992 to provide retail space known as Spires Mall on the ground floor, which has since closed. The grand Main Hall is used as a conference venue.

37. GRAND OPERA HOUSE

The wonderful Grand Opera House (left) was designed by leading English theatre architect Frank Matcham and opened in 1895 in Great Victoria Street at what was then a desirable residential location. It was described at the time as a 'perfect Eastern palace'. In 1963 Pavarotti made his British debut at the Grand Opera House, playing Lieutenant Pinkerton in *Madame Butterfly*. In view alongside the Grand Opera House are the Hippodrome cinema, and in the distance is the Municipal Technical Institute, which were both built in 1907. In between, the huge Ritz cinema (now the site of Jury's Hotel) was opened in 1936 when Gracie Fields took part in the opening ceremony.

38. GREAT NORTHERN RAILWAY STATION

The Great Northern Railway (GNR) station on Great Victoria Street was opened in 1848 and its imposing façade (seen here) containing twelve Doric columns has been described as 'pompous'. My grandfather Billy Walker was freight superintendent of the GNR in the 1950s and his office was in the building to the far right. The GNR was originally known as the Ulster Railway and heralded the first railway line in Belfast, which travelled 7½ miles to Lisburn in 1837. The station was directly opposite the Crown Bar, which was made famous by the 1947 Carol Reed film *Odd Man Out* starring James Mason. In 1971 Great Victoria Street station was replaced by the Europa Hotel, known as 'Europe's most bombed hotel'.

39. SHAFTESBURY SQUARE

Shaftesbury Square is a major road junction that connects the city centre with south Belfast. The name originates from the time when the 8th Earl of Shaftesbury married Lady Harriet Chichester on 22 August 1857. She was the only daughter of George Hamilton Chichester, 3rd Marquis of Donegall, whose family had founded Belfast in the 1600s, and this happy event apparently restored the Donegall family fortunes. This was once a residential area at the junction of Great Victoria Street and Dublin Road and in the 1870s the houses had front gardens with railings, although today it is mostly restaurants and offices.

40. CRESCENT ARTS CENTRE

Upper and Lower Crescents were completed with grand housing in the 1850s, containing 'highly imposing stucco terraces in the Bath manner'. At No. 1 University Road (seen here), on the corner of Lower Crescent, stands the current Crescent Arts Centre, which during major renovations was awarded the UK 'Man and the Biosphere' Urban Wildlife Award for Excellence in 2010 for preserving the 136-year-old breeding colony of threatened swifts. This was once the home of Victoria College, Belfast's premier girls' grammar school, which was founded by Mrs Margaret Byers in 1859 and moved to Lower Crescent in 1873. Queen Victoria graciously granted the royal title in 1870.

THE ULSTER HOUSE OF PARLIAMENT, BELFAST. 166.

41. UNION THEOLOGICAL COLLEGE

The architect of Assembly's College (now Union Theological College) on Botanic Avenue (seen here) was Charles Lanyon and it was founded in 1853 by the General Assembly of the Presbyterian Church in Ireland to provide training for Presbyterian ministers. The façade has a grand Doric porch in rusticated stonework and the building was once described as 'the finest architectural edifice in Belfast'. From 1921 to 1932 the newly formed Parliament of Northern Ireland met in Assembly's College while awaiting the construction of the new Parliament Buildings at Stormont.

42. QUEEN'S UNIVERSITY

Queen's College Belfast (now Queen's University) was opened in 1849 (along with Queen's Colleges in Cork and Galway), thus giving a tremendous stimulus to the intellectual life of Belfast. It was inspected just before opening by Queen Victoria and Prince Albert, who was nominated as first chancellor but respectfully declined. Queen's was designed by the architect Charles Lanyon and modelled on Magdalen College, Oxford, in the Tudor revival style, which represented ancient learning and scholarly tradition. It has been described as 'one of the principal ornaments of Belfast'.

43. BOTANIC GARDENS ENTRANCE

The ornate Ruskinian or Venetian Gothic-style gate lodge with a clock tower was designed by architect William Batt in the 1870s and built in a mixture of brick and stone. It stood at the entrance to Botanic Gardens, but was 'wantonly demolished' in 1965, making the site now seem rather empty. The large house standing at the junction of University, Stranmillis and Malone Roads behind the tram was built in 1889 and is remarkably unchanged. The electric tram is an early model that included an upstairs roof to protect passengers from the weather.

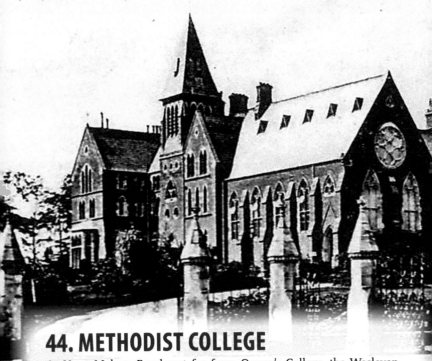

44. METHODIST COLLEGE

At No. 1 Malone Road, not far from Queen's College, the Wesleyan Methodist Collegiate Institution was opened in 1868 (seen here) bordering the countryside and surrounded by fields and the occasional farm. The grand school buildings were designed in the Victorian Gothic and other historic styles. Despite its name, the school had the dual purpose of training candidates for the Methodist ministry as well as a general education for boys and girls of any denomination. It became known as Methodist College Belfast in 1885 and, more recently, was my old school.

45. ULSTER MUSEUM

The Belfast Natural History and Philosophical Society was founded in 1821, and in 1830 the enthusiastic membership built a new museum in the fashionable area of College Square North, overlooking Inst school. In those self-reliant times the museum was the first in Ireland to be built by voluntary subscriptions. In 1929 it moved to its present location (seen here) on Stranmillis Road. A major extension to the original museum building was completed in 1964 and described as a 'deft union of two diametrically opposed building styles'. A more recent renovation was completed in 2009 and the museum reopened on its 80th anniversary.

46. PALM HOUSE BOTANIC GARDENS

The Belfast Botanical and Horticultural Society established the Botanic Gardens as a private concern from public subscriptions in 1828. The Marquis of Donegall laid the foundation stone for the world's first curvilinear glass and iron Palm House (pictured) in 1839 (predating the Palm House at Kew Gardens) and this was followed in 1889 by a new Tropical Ravine building, with a sunken glen and a waterfall. The gardens held many social activities during Victorian times including band concerts, military tournaments, dog shows and tightrope walking. Botanic Gardens was sold to Belfast Corporation in 1895, when they were opened, free of charge, to the general public and became Belfast's sixth public park. Dublin-born glasshouse designer and ironfounder Richard Turner built both the Belfast and Kew Gardens palm houses.

47. FRIAR'S BUSH GRAVEYARD

In the distance is the towering 'wedding cake' presence of Elmwood Presbyterian Church. The open-topped tram on the Stranmillis Road indicates a date of around 1907. Friar's Bush is the oldest burial ground in Belfast and is immediately to the right. Its gate lodge has been described as 'a miniature Westminster Abbey' and it was once the site of a Franciscan monastery. Friar's Bush was the main Roman Catholic burial ground in Belfast until 1869 when Milltown Cemetery was opened on Falls Road. In 1928 the Marquis of Donegall provided land for an extension to the Friar's Bush site, and an 8-foot-high wall was erected to deter bodysnatchers.

48. THE WORKHOUSE

Following a number of fever epidemics in the 1830s, the Irish Poor Relief Act of 1838 established the Belfast Union Workhouse on the Lisburn Road, which had room for 1,000 people (seen here). It was once described as 'gloomy'. The Belfast Union Fever Hospital was added in 1865. When the Poor Law system was closed down in 1948 these buildings came under the auspices of the Hospital Authority and were demolished to accommodate the site of the new Belfast City Hospital tower block in 1984. In 2015 surgeons at Belfast City Hospital carried out five kidney transplants in a single day to equal a UK record.

49. KING'S HALL, BALMORAL

The Royal Ulster Agricultural Society was based at the markets in Belfast, and in 1896 moved to a new 32-acre site at Balmoral. The King's Hall (seen here) became the centrepiece building of the complex, and it dominates this 1940s view. It was built in 1934 and opened by the Duke of Gloucester. For many years it was Northern Ireland's largest exhibition centre and concert venue until the more recent opening of the Odyssey and the Waterfront Hall. It closed in 2012 and there have been recent newspaper reports that the King's Hall complex is to be redeveloped.

50. SHAW'S BRIDGE

Shaw's Bridge is a stone structure with five arches that spans the River Lagan, as in this idyllic rural 1930s view with cattle and barge. In 1655 Captain Shaw, in Oliver Cromwell's army, built a strong wooden bridge capable of carrying heavy siege artillery, but this was washed away in a storm and a five-arched stone bridge replaced it in 1709. The Lagan Canal opened in 1763 to connect Belfast with Lough Neagh and closed in the 1950s, unable to compete with faster road traffic. The old bridge has been retained and is now part of a pedestrian area in the picturesque 4,000-acre Lagan Valley Regional Park.